The
SPUR BOOK
of
HILL TREKKING

by
Peter Lumley

SPURBOOKS LIMITED

Published 1977 by
Spurbooks Ltd.
6 Parade Court
Bourne End
Bucks

ISBN 0 904978 22 2

CONTENTS

PUBLISHER'S INTRODUCTION

Venture Guides aim to provide outdoor enthusiasts, and all those involved in active leisure pastimes, with a range of knowledge on which to base their activities.

For, whatever the particular activity, climbing, camping, rambling, sailing or whatever, the outdoor man or woman needs to have a grounding in outdoor techniques, such as Knot Tying, Boat Handling, Weather Lore, Camping Skills, Map and Compass Work, Outdoor First Aid, Ski-ing, Rock Climbing, Backpacking, and now, in the subject of this book, Hill-Trekking.

ABOUT THIS BOOK

Do people go walking in the hills to find peace and quiet, or is it for the physical challenge that walking on the high ground can give? Perhaps it is just for the view! No matter how good the scenery is along the valley floor, it is always much better when seen from lofty heights. Whatever the reason, trekking in the hills is a growing sport.

Britain is not a mountainous country if compared with Switzerland, Sweden, Norway or France, but our mountains are nearer our cities, and often accessible for day-walking or for weekend treks. They are not as high as the Continental ones, but they are no less dangerous when the weather closes down, when you take unnecessary risks, or travel without the necessary equipment and experience.

WHERE TO GO

In the British Isles we classify hills over 2,000 feet as mountains. Only in the extreme South-Coastal and Home Counties areas are we very far from high ground. Even then it is not too far to the Brecon Beacons, the Black Mountains of Wales, or the Peak District of Derbyshire. There is high and open ground also, in Scotland, the Lake District, Yorkshire, and on Exmoor and Dartmoor. All of these are good areas for hill-trekking (Figure 1).

This book is about walking in the hills and wild places of Britain, and about finding your way around them safely, planning trips away from the pavements and streets of our towns and cities. Hill-trekking can bridge the gap between rambling and mountaineering, while having special attractions of its own.

This book explains the basics of trekking in the hills, the equipment to wear, and essential items to carry, the risks one must beware of and the knowledge necessary to minimize them. It is hoped that this book will enable the beginner to know and enjoy the special attractions of hill-trekking.

I would like to thank Rob Hunter and Terry Brown for the use of extracts from their books on First-Aid, Map and Compass, and Weather Lore, also published in this series, and Terry Brown especially for the illustrations, not forgetting the many back-packers and hill-trekkers who, over the years, have added their experience to mine.

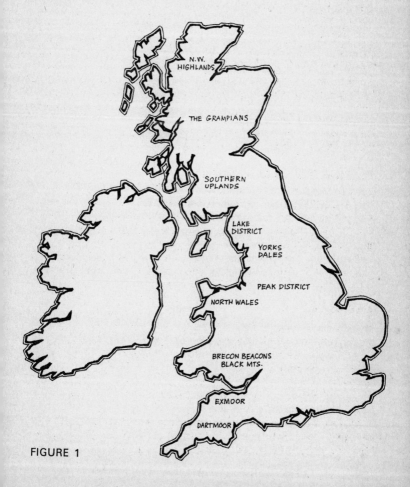

FIGURE 1

Chapter 1

SAFETY AND THE COUNTRY CODE

There is, of course, an element of risk when going into the hills. Our lives are full of risks, even lower down the valley. Realising and acknowledging that risks exist, is more than half the battle towards minimizing the danger.

BE SAFETY MINDED

On British hills you won't need to worry about grizzly bears or man-eating lions, but there is always a threat from wind and rain, from cold and fog. Weather patterns change, often in minutes. What started as a pleasant day can quickly turn into the worst weather you have ever known. Wind and wet spell danger, so that keeping warm and dry is imperative. If you cannot keep dry then to minimise the effect of being wet by wearing windproofs becomes even more important. Do not, however, change into dry clothes every time you get wet, or you will end your day with a rucksack full of wet clothes. And that's heavy!

ACCIDENTS CAN HAPPEN

A sprained ankle can turn even a short walk into a nightmare marathon. Other injuries, minor or otherwise, no matter how they are sustained, can be even more of a problem when in the hills. The most feared danger of all is exposure. Exposure is the creeping chill which numbs your mind and creeps into your body surreptitiously. It leaves the senses unaware that danger is upon you. Watch out then, especially, for exposure symptoms, and let's look at them now.

EXPOSURE

Symptoms of exposure are not always easy to spot, but in general terms they show up in uncharacteristic behaviour. Exposure will bring on complaints of coldness and tiredness, yet the sufferer often gives outbursts of violent effort, and equally violent language! Stumbling and falling down, chattering or, alternatively, appearing morose, may all indicate exposure, if this is uncharacteristic behaviour on a *cold, wet day*.

Exposure is so serious that it must be treated the moment it is spotted. That is one reason for *always* carrying spare, dry clothing. The patient must be sheltered and warmed up as fast as possible. Experienced walkers treat the high-outdoors with respect and avoid going into the hills with anything less than the proper equipment. The beginner must do the same. The right equipment is described in this book, but a maxim to remember is:

Think before each step what the consequences might be.

I shall return regularly to safety points throughout this book.

THE COUNTRY CODE

Whether you go on to the hills in company with others, who can show you the right behaviour, or are learning step by step, remember that the Countryside Code matters. It is a simple, ten-point creed:—

> Guard against all risks of fire.
> Fasten all gates.
> Keep dogs under proper control.
> Keep to paths across farmland.
> Avoid damaging fences, walls and hedges.
> Leave no litter.
> Safeguard all water supplies.
> Protect wild life, plants and trees.
> Go carefully when on country roads.
> Respect the life of the countryside.

Chapter 2

MENTAL AND PHYSICAL FITNESS, COMPANIONSHIP, PRECAUTIONS

To get the utmost enjoyment from any activity, be it ski-ing or skittles, you have to have the right attitude of mind.

BE PHYSICALLY AND MENTALLY FIT

Hill-walking calls for certain qualities and attitudes, and if, for example, you are the sort of person who prefers to ride escalators or lifts rather than walk up the stairs, then perhaps you won't take to life in the hills. You have to *enjoy* the effort that the hills demand, and be able to force yourself to the finish, when you may feel that you would rather stop.

If physical exercise is something you have never been interested in, and have no experience of, then don't rush into the high hills right away. Make sure you have the stamina to put one foot in front of the other for hours over difficult terrain. Hill-walking is something which ought to follow automatically once you have got used to trotting around low-level footpaths, where the gradient is not too much of an extra burden over the distance. Hill-walking, of the kind discussed here, is not necessarily only for super-fit athletes, but it is a pastime which requires stamina. Running is an excellent exercise for building up stamina and getting the legs fit. Eventually the hills themselves will toughen you. That will come in time, but to start with, think about companionship, because the hills can be very lonely, especially if you run into some sort of trouble. Unless you are *very* experienced, you should not go into the hills on your own in anything but the mildest weather, and even then you should keep low down, and away from the heights.

PICKING A COMPANION

Finding a companion for a bash in the hills is far from easy. People walk at different speeds, and even those of us who walk along a street at the same speed, may have far different rates of ascent and descent when in the hills. For that reason you have to pick your companions with care, and they—and you for that matter— must have a firm understanding of what you are going to do, what you enjoy, who pays for what, and who does what, and when. It all boils down to getting on well together, and having a sense of humour. Having different interests may be an advantage, especially if one member knows all about the birds (feathered variety) and another has a botanical interest. Botany, geology, and ornithology, are good interests for hill-walkers.

When there are more than two of you in a party, remember that it is important to have one leader and one person keeping tabs at the rear so that slow friends are not forgotten or left behind. Always travel at the speed of the slowest in the party, although it can be very irritating if one person is a natural slow-coach. A few short trips would be advisable to make quite sure that you can get on together when it gets rough.

There are times of the year when it may be positively dangerous for people to go into the hills, however experienced they may be. These are when the weather is obviously going to be so bad that conditions will leave you feeling wretched, or when snow and ice make walking very difficult. These are the times when you need wise counsel and reliable companionship. There will also be occasions when bad weather conditions will creep up on you unawares. Never neglect to study the weather, and always take the appropriate equipment. Finally, how do you react to challenge? This is a question to be answered truthfully, because if, for example, you are the type who panics easily, then you must avoid putting yourself in a situation where panic can occur. There is no way to control the elements, or to have adventures trekking into the hills, without some risk to you or your companions, but the risks can usually be calculated.

DON'T LEAVE YOUR SAFETY TO OTHERS

When you set out to walk into the hills, imagine that you, and only you, are going. Do not leave essential items of equipment, first-aid, or food, for others to carry. Look to your own needs and make sure that in the event of a mishap *you* are able to cope with an accident on your own, before it develops into a serious emergency. Above all, never set out without leaving word of your whereabouts. Take the following precautions—ALWAYS:—

1. Decide upon your route.
2. Estimate the time you will be away, and where you will stop if it is necessary.
3. Jot as much information as possible down on a route card, to be left with someone, or attach it in a prominent position on your vehicle.
4. Know where the nearest telephones are on your chosen route, and the location of rescue posts or rescue parties, together with the location of the nearest medical aid, i.e. doctors.

5. Check that you have an adequate first-aid and survival pack, for whatever trip you have in mind.

If trouble does beset you all these will be important links to help you survive and help any rescue service trying to reach you. Attention to these points may save your life. Make such precautions a drill, something you do always, every time, not just now and again (Figure 2).

FIGURE 2

Chapter 3

EQUIPMENT, CLOTHING AND FOOD

People *do* walk into high hills in city suits, town shoes and with nothing more in wet-weather-wear than a brolly. Mountain Rescue teams find them all the time! People like this are taking a risk that *you* would not want to take, and such people are very lucky if they escape safe and sound. Those who have done so, or those of your friends who regularly 'get away with it', may wonder why such a fuss is made about not wearing cotton jeans in winter, or why you need a spare woollen jumper, rainwear and leggings. It's all very simple. The risk is there and one day they are going to get caught out.

Take the right gear. You will be warmer, drier, and safer. I'm sorry to labour the safety point, but the hills are perfectly safe as long as you remember the dangers you *may* have to face and are ready for them. The most potent of these dangers is *weather*, so again, let's look at it briefly here.

WEATHER FACTORS

Weather can, and does, change very quickly. It is also important to realise that what may be a warm summer day down on the valley floor, is almost certainly going to be a chilly (or chillier) one higher up. The higher you go, the quicker conditions can change. Wind is the biggest enemy. It will chill you, and do so faster as the wind-speed increases.

Rain increases the adverse effects of wind. It also restricts visibility, often to a dangerous limit. A hill-mist can damp you down and get you lost, and at such times you will need to use the compass constantly. Darkness comes down quickly in autumn and winter. It is important to know sunset times and estimate the duration of your journey, so that you do not run out of time and get caught out after dark. Weather changes the terrain, and the nature of the ground beneath your feet.

Your clothing and equipment must take account of *all* these factors, in the items you carry, and the use you may have to find for them. In everything you buy, remember the **weight,** for heavy loads can exhaust you easily.

CLOTHING

Garments which trap pockets of air close to your body will keep you warm, providing you have outer clothing to keep that air in place. Several layers of thin clothing are better than one thick one.

Do not wear nylon shirts or underwear—wool is best, especially in winter. An absorbent garment, again preferably wool, will keep you very warm when worn next to the skin. A string vest is a good idea for summer wear. Cover this with a wool shirt (or shirts) if the weather is cold. Two thin shirts are better than one —again, because they will trap layers or pockets of air, and these air layers keep the warmth in and the cold out (Figure 3).

Wear two thin woollen sweaters rather than one thick one. Temperature control is then easier, for, let it not be forgotten, you can also get too hot.

These garments will have little effect in stopping fierce cold winds cutting through to you, so you need something such as a Ventile jacket or a cotton-twill smock as top wear. Nylon, especially proofed nylon, would not be very suitable, because the body heat built up inside will create condensation (or moisture) inside the nylon, which coupled with the wind, will chill you, even more so that the effects of the wind by itself. Wool underneath, in layers, and a Ventile jacket or smock on top, is the answer. If you wear an anorak be sure it is big enough to get warm clothes on underneath it.

WATERPROOFS

To keep out wet weather you need a cagoule or a waterproof jacket. Such a garment, with a front zip, will allow the ventilation to be adjusted, thus minimising condensation. The zips should have a baffle to prevent water seeping or being driven through the zip. A cagoule needs to be long enough to give adequate protection against the weather. A further advantage of cagoules is that they are usually very light to wear. A cagoule made from nylon will have a proofing surface applied to the surface. This will eventually be ruined by the constant rubbing of belts and the shoulder-straps of rucksacks. Careless packing in a rucksack could also spoil these garments. Be sure to dry them, and fold them neatly. At home, cagoules should be hung up on hangers. In most conditions, but especially in cold weather, a waterproof nylon cagoule will generate a great deal of condensation on the inside. This condensation can seep into your inner clothing and, when coupled with a cold wind, will cause rapid chilling. There-

FIGURE 3

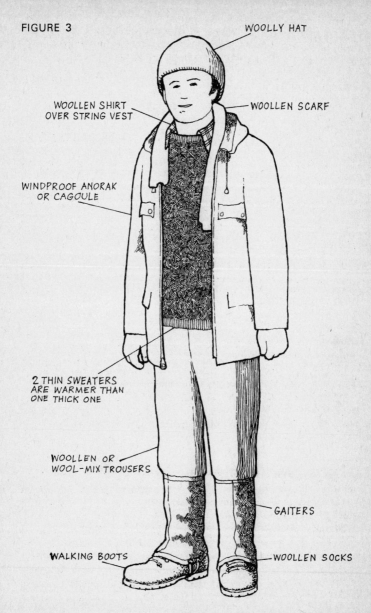

WOOLLY HAT

WOOLLEN SHIRT
OVER STRING VEST

WOOLLEN SCARF

WINDPROOF ANORAK
OR CAGOULE

2 THIN SWEATERS
ARE WARMER THAN
ONE THICK ONE

WOOLLEN OR
WOOL-MIX TROUSERS

GAITERS

WALKING BOOTS

WOOLLEN SOCKS

fore, keep the cagoule open at every opportunity, or have one with a suitable lining. Having a lined waterproof garment can reduce the level of condensation to an acceptable degree.

TROUSERS

You do not need trousers which are specially made for the job of hill-trekking, although plus-fours, or breeches, look smart and are very functional. Close-cut trousers will restrict leg movement, especially when stepping upwards among rocks or boulders. Wide-legged trousers can be very heavy when wet and are difficult to fit inside gaiters.

Jeans, cotton cords, and light man-made fibre trousers are not suitable for wearing in the hills, as they hold little warmth when wet, and are often uncomfortable to walk in. Wear a wool or wool mix pair, and be sure they are comfortable.

You can buy a pair of waterproof over-trousers and these should either extend to ankle length, or be long enough to fit into the tops of your gaiters. This will give toe-to-hip protection and, coupled with a cagoule, will mean that you have head-to-toe waterproofing.

GAITERS

The leggings which fit over your boot and extend part way to the knee are called gaiters, and serve several functions, the most important one being to keep your legs and ankles dry and clean. Gaiters will be worn nearly all the time when you are walking in wet or peaty hills. If conditions underfoot are wet or muddy, then the gaiters will make sure your boot tops do not sink under the mire. They also help when you have to ford a stream.

GLOVES AND HEADWEAR

Woollen gloves, or mittens, are necessary to keep your hands warm in winter, and even in summer in cold, windy weather. In really bad conditions, waterproof over-mitts should be worn.

The head is your body's radiator. If you are feeling cold, put on your hat. For hill-walking, the woollen balaclava is ideal, or you could use a simple wool ski-hat. Another good idea is to use a woollen scarf, or dish-towel, tied lightly round the neck, which is an alternative way of making trapped warm air stay with you, and when it rains the scarf stops the water running down your neck.

SOCKS

There is nothing better than wool when it comes to socks. The ones you will use will probably have a small amount of nylon reinforcement at the toe and heel. A spare pair of socks is very useful if you get wet feet when crossing a stream or after a full day walking on wet ground. If your feet and head feel warm, all of you seems to feel warm. Be sure the socks are well washed and soft. New socks can cause blisters.

BOOTS OR SHOES?

Boots are really essential, although a good pair of stoutly-made shoes, with a thick patterned sole, would be all right providing you always keep to a good path. However, it's safer to be prepared for the unexpected detour over rougher ground, and wear boots. These should be broad enough and fit well. The sole and heel pattern is most important, for if the soles are worn and rounded, the grip will not be sufficient in poor ground conditions. When walking downhill a lot of problems show up with boots and feet, because you will find that sore feet develop much more quickly going downhill than toiling uphill. The weight of your body and pack are all thrust down on to the feet and toes.

A typical sole-pattern on boots is the Vibram, which has a ribbed, or cleated design, which gives a good grip on dry mud, rock and grass, but it is not so good in the wet. Vibram soles should be renewed if there is excessive smoothing down of the sole and heel pattern. All good walking boots can be re-soled and you shoud have this done *before* they get smooth and therefore dangerous (Figure 4).

Remember that a twisted ankle in a desolate spot could mean much more than inconvenience for you, your companions, or anyone else involved, such as the rescue teams, so look with particular care at feet and footwear.

FIGURE 4

WALKING BOOT

VIBRAM SOLE

Footwear is an extremely important item, for it represents your only contact with the ground, and if you have unsure footing, then you. are quite likely to suffer some mishap. It is false economy to go trekking in the hills without the correct footwear. Nailed boots are safer in winter, or when on muddy slopes.

CARRYING IT ALL

For a day trek you will need a small rucksack or haversack to carry spare clothing, waterproofs and emergency kit. Include some food and a flask of hot drink for use during the day.

Don't waste money on a large rucksack, or one which has a frame if you intend only to involve yourself with short day walks. The larger versions are for treks lasting two or more days, when you will also need a tent, sleeping gear, food and a cooking stove.

MAP AND COMPASS

The best type of compass is the *Silva*. These can be bought in several versions, one of which has a magnified, luminous, dis-mountable dial, for use as a wrist compass. There are other makes, but this is the best-known and the most popular among people who go into the hills. They cost between £5 and £12.

Your map, or maps, have to be large-scale sheets, covering the **total** area you are visiting. Ordnance Survey maps are expensive, but they are the best you can buy. Any scale smaller than 1 : 50,000 is not much use in hilly country, unless the path is waymarked, and in some remote areas 1 : 25,000 is better still (Figure 5).

Keep your maps clean and dry (for as long as possible) by using a plastic cover. A stout plastic bag is a good alternative if you have not been able to obtain a plastic map case.

Coating the map with clear adhesive film is a useful idea which will prolong the life of the map considerably, but remember, maps and compass are just extra weight unless you know how to use them. (See Chapter 4).

FIRST-AID KIT

You will need a few plasters, cottonwool, "moleskin" (for blisters), and antiseptic cream. Scissors, Aspirin, a 2" bandage, one or two safety pins (which also come in handy for torn clothing), and a few large squares of lint or gauze. You can expand this kit as much as you like. Buy the Spur Book of First Aid, and learn about the subject.

TORCH AND WHISTLE: EMERGENCY SIGNALS

Even if you do not intend to stay out after dark, it pays to take a torch with you. You never know what may happen! The torch should be one with a good spread of light so that following a path would be reasonably easy. Batteries should obviously be new, or nearly so, and they must also be able to sustain a good light for at least two hours continuous use. Carry spare batteries and bulbs.

To save a short circuit or switch fault wasting the batteries, it is a good idea to reverse them in the torch case so that the light will not work until needed.

Never blow a whistle unless you are in danger or are answering another call. Never flash a light around unnecessarily when in the hills. It is an important safety link which should not be abused. The distress signal is six blasts on the whistle, followed by a minute's silence. Then repeat. With a torch it is six flashes, pause, then repeat.

SURVIVAL KIT

Even a day trip *could* lead you to being stuck out overnight. If you have:—
1. A sheet of plastic or polythene 10' x 4'
2. A space blanket
3. Some chocolate or biscuits,
you can be sheltered, warm, and fed, for at least one night, and these items weigh very little and can be stored with your clothes in your rucksack. They may save you much misery, and *always* take them with you. If you don't have them already, buy them now, and put in the rucksack.

FIGURE 5

Chapter 4

MAP AND COMPASS

Old saying:

> *The man who knows where he is going*
> *never asks the way.*

This is a very important saying, so remember it. Know where you are going, where you are now, and where you have been. This is extremely important in the hills as rain or mist can cut your visibility in a few minutes, and there is usually no-one to ask anyway.

Many people who go into the hills simply arrive at a car park, scratch through the glove compartment for a map, and set out. They rely on the fact that the path is well-trodden, with a few discarded beer cans, a cigarette packet or two, several sweet wrappers, and usually some cairns, all marking the way.

Cairns are little heaps—or even big heaps—of stones, which are piled up to show you the path. In mist or snowy conditions they are very useful. They also mark the path through really rocky areas, and are a common sight on most of the hills in the Lake District, in Scotland, and along the Pennine Way. You may see them wherever there is a path. But sometimes there are so many you will be confused, which is another reason why you need a map and compass, which you must know how to use.

THE MAP

In most cases you will be using the 1 : 50,000 series, Ordnance Survey maps, which are expensive but very good. There are 204 sheets, covering the whole of the British Isles, including the Shetlands, Orkneys and Outer Hebrides. Folded, and with a thick cover, the current price is £1.15 per sheet. Bought flat, without the cover, they cost at present 80p.

In the hills, you need to read contour lines be able to identify one hill or feature among many, and be able to identify natural as opposed to man-made features on the ground. Can you tell a spur from a re-entrant off the map? Well, you should. You must be able to feel the 'tilt' of the land, and always keep the map 'set' or 'oriented'. Never go out without a local map and compass in your possession.

The O.S. map uses symbols and marks devised to indicate everything from a public house to an old mine-working. Learn your contours and symbols until you can read a map like any book, but the first point to note is the Magnetic Variations, and the next thing to do is to 'set' the map, that is, to line up features on the map with the features they represent on the ground.

MAP REFERENCES

Map references are usually given in six-figure numbers, representing the grid square, and a particular point within that square. The map is criss-crossed with vertical and horizontal grid lines. Each line is identified by a two-figure number, and these give you the first of the numbers of each map reference—two vertical numbers and two horizontal numbers (Figure 6).

The vertical lines are known as 'eastings', for although they run, individually, up and down the map, they advance in series across the map from left to right, or heading from west to east—hence 'eastings'.

The same applies to the horizontal lines which advance in series

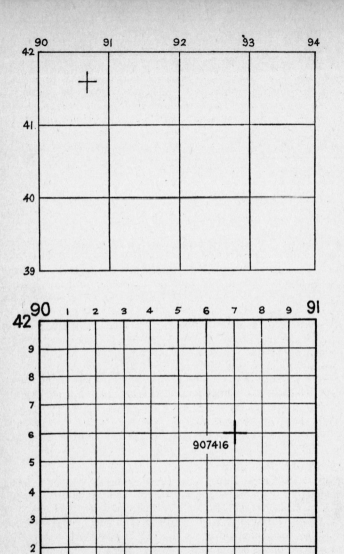

FIGURE 6

Grid on map references

up the map, from south to north, and are called 'northings'.

Where two lines intersect you have a grid point, and you can express this by giving the numbers of the grid lines to indicate the bottom left-hand corner of the relevant grid square. Then, to find the point you require within the square, you divide the 'eastings' and 'northings' lines into ten, and pinpoint the spot by referring to the intersection of the imaginary lines which would cut it. With practice you can get these tenths estimated very easily. Otherwise, to be more accurate, you can use the millimetre scale on your Silva compass. Each side of the grid square means 20 mm, so 2 mm is $\frac{1}{10}$ of the line. Try it and see. You can also make yourself a 'roamer', or purchase a plastic one of the right scale in a sports shop.

This sounds complicated, but is in fact quite simple. The point to remember is to give the map reference in the correct order. The correct order is to give the 'easting' three-figure reference, first. Remember the 'eastings' are the **vertical** lines which run in series **across** the map.

Then give the 'northing' three-figure reference. These are the **horizontal** lines which run **up** the map. Put together you have a six-figure map reference with which to locate any spot on the map that you require.

The rule then, is 'eastings' before 'northings'. You can remember this by recalling that 'E' comes before 'N' in the alphabet, or by the mental reminder that when giving a map reference you **go along the corridor, then up the stairs.**

You will, not infrequently, both give and receive incorrect map references, where the eastings and northings have been reversed. It is a common error, so look out for it.

SETTING THE MAP BY THE COMPASS

This is a useful skill if you are in mountains, hills, or on a featureless plain. You need to know where North lies in order to 'set' the map. First set the magnetic variation on the compass. Then place the compass on the map with the compass needle to north and turn the **map** until the orienting lines (on the compass) lie parallel to the **grid** lines (on the map). Now you know which way you are facing, the direction of North, and can start to try and identify points on the ground from the map, or vice-versa.

The compass is a delicate instrument, which, basically, indicates the position of Magnetic North. From this basic point, a number of deductions and uses follow. You need to know 'magnetic' north in order to 'set' a map properly at times when you cannot 'set' it by aligning it with physical features. At other times, however, you ought to be able to locate your position by reading the map and identifying the features around you. The compass can be used to verify your findings, by taking bearings on notable features.

'Setting' or orienting the map means that you line up the map features with the physical features which they identify on the ground. Have you got that?

Compasses are delicate, but that does not mean that they cannot withstand knocks and bangs. What a compass does not like is magnetic influences, like those arising from being left on top of the T.V. set at home, or from being put near a transistor radio. You should always keep it well away from your watch, car or motor cycle engine, or metal objects.

The summits of many hills are marked by triangulation points. These are concrete obelisks on which instruments are put when surveying work is in progress. The metal fittings on these trig points can affect the reading given by your compass. So beware!

CONTOURS

A map is a pictorial representation of the ground, but while the map is flat, the ground is bumpy; not to mention rolling, hilly or mountainous. These changes in the level, or relief of the land are indicated on O.S. maps by contour lines.

Contours are quite easy to follow, provided you grasp the idea that a contour is an imaginary line following the surface of the ground at a specific level. The contour follows the same height, round the hills, into the re-entrants, and over the spurs. Contours make no effort to indicate the relief, but they can give you a very good idea of the shape of the land. On the 1 : 50,000 O.S. map the contour lines are 50 feet apart. Therefore, if the lines are close together it follows that the land is rising very quickly. If far apart, that the slope is gentle. If at irregular intervals that the land undulates (Figure 7).

One point that foxes people is to know from the contour lines whether the land is rising or falling, whether a feature is a spur or re-entrant. A spur projects from the land mass, while a re-entrant is exactly the opposite i.e., a shallow valley reaching into the mass. Apart from experience, these points will help. Firstly, the contour values, which are given to the nearest **metre**, are given so that they read facing uphill. Remember, though, that while the heights are given in metres, the contour lines are 50

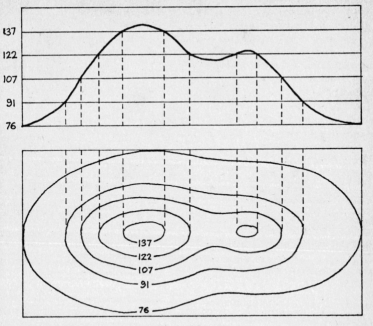

CONTOURS OF A HILL WITH A COL

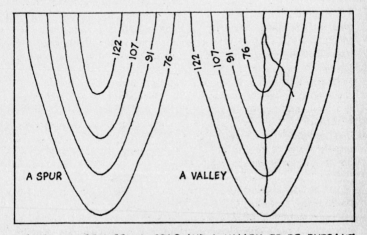

A SPUR   A VALLEY

DIFFERENCE BETWEEN A SPUR AND A VALLEY OR RE-ENTRANT

FIGURE 7   Contour lines

feet apart. Secondly, you can compare contour values which are given at regular intervals along the line. Thirdly, common sense. Rivers and streams do not normally run up spurs or along the tops of hills. Often other features will give you the clue.

Apart from contours, height is indicated by **spot heights** which are indicated on the map as follows: °117. This is the precise height, in metres, above sea level at this particular point. You will also find **trig points**, indicated on the map as follows: △ 180. This again is the exact height above sea level.

Finally, apart from contour lines, very steep slopes or cliffs are shown by a visual reproduction of a cliff, or a series of sharp jagged arrow-heads. Be wary of areas like this when out on the ground.

FINDING YOUR POSITION BY COMPASS— RESECTION

To find your position you need two or more identifiable features or landmarks on the ground that you can also find on the map. These should preferably be some distance apart, at right-angles to each other, so that you have cross-bearings to fix your position. This is called 're-section'.

You may know where your landmarks are on the map and ground but you don't know where *you* are. To find out, take the following action.

Take the Silva compass in the left hand and point the Travel arrow directly at the landmark. Then, holding the compass steady, swivel the compass housing until the needle and orienting arrow match, North to North. The bearing of the landmark can now be read off the dial at the Index pointer mark. Note this bearing down.

Repeat this with the second and subsequent landmarks, until you have two or more **magnetic** bearings, from your position to two identifiable landmarks.

Note this carefully: These are **magnetic** or compass bearings. They need to be converted into **grid** bearings by removing the **magnetic variation**. To convert a magnetic bearing to a grid bearing you subtract the variation.

Magnetic **U**nto **G**rid = **S**ubtract

The magnetic variation is the amount by which magnetic North differs from Grid North.

This mnemonic, MUGS, from the first letter of each word is one way of remembering what to do to convert bearings. People frequently make mistakes in converting bearings, and this may help you to get it right.

In the present case we have to subtract the magnetic variation from the magnetic bearing to get a grid bearing. So, if our magnetic bearings were 300° and 50° respectively, and the magnetic variation was 8°, our grid bearings would be 292° and 42° respectively.

These are bearings from your position to the landmarks, from a point you cannot identify to two (or more) points you *can* identify. You can find your position as follows:

Set the first magnetic bearing on the dial of the compass, and then deduct the variation. This automatically gives you the grid bearing. Forget the compass bearing, you no longer need it. Place the compass on the map. Place the direction line over the first landmark, with the landmark as close to the compass dial as possible. Then, keeping the sighting line over the landmark, swivel the compass until the **orienting lines** are parallel with the **grid lines**, with the orienting arrow pointing North. Next, at the point where the sighting line runs off the compass, mark the map with a dot, making a map mark.

Now, using the edge of the compass as a ruler, draw a pencil line connecting the map mark and the landmark, and run it back towards you. Your position is somwhere along that line.

Repeat the process on the second landmark. The line from this point should cut the first line, and where they cut, is your position.

Remember the steps:—

1. Identify two or more landmarks on the ground and on the map.
2. Take magnetic bearings.
3. Deduct the magnetic variation to make a grid bearing.
4. Set these bearings on the compass and draw in a series of intersecting lines on the map.
5. Where the lines intersect is your position.

COMPASS MARCHING

You must also be able to work out a bearing off the map, add the magnetic variation to get a compass bearing, and march on it, even at night or in mist. You need to know the difference between magnetic, grid and true North.

To obtain a grid bearing you have first to identify your position and your objective on the map. Lay the edge of the Silva compass down as a line to connect these two points, then turn the compass housing until the orienting lines are parallel to the grid lines. Ignore the compass needle at this point. You can now read off the grid bearing at the index pointer. Rememebr this is a 'grid' bearing and to convert it into a **magnetic** or **compass** bearing, you have to **add** the magnetic variation, i.e., **G**rid **U**nto **M**agnetic **A**dd, or **GUMA**. This mnemonic will help you remember what to do. Let us say that again the magnetic variation is 8°, so if your grid bearing is 250, you add 8, and set the compass dial to 258°.

You can now put the map away, and taking the compass in the left hand, simply swivel yourself around, until the North point of the compass needle centres over the North point of the orienting arrow. To march in the correct direction, (258°) you keep these needles together and start off in the direction indicated by the travel arrow.

To be able to march on a compass bearing is the real crux of map and compass work; in the hills, the process of calculating a bearing on a map, translating it on to the compass, and then, using both compass and map, marching to, and arriving at your destination easily and safely, in all weathers, by day or night, is a vital hill-trekking skill.

Keep your compass on a neck-cord or elastic so that it is handy for use when required. A lost compass could be a disaster and if you are travelling for several days it is a good idea to have a second one tied inside your rucksack. You may lose your compass easily, but few people would lose a rucksack without noticing it!

The 'Spur Book of Map and Compass', published in this series, will tell you much more about how to read a map and find your way across country.

HOW FAR TO GO

Deciding the length of your walk into the hills depends a lot on such factors as how much time you have available, the time of year, what the weather is like, and how difficult is the terrain.

Always check the weather forecast before making up your mind to go into the hills. Bad weather will make an easy walk difficult, and a hard trek impossible.

On the valley floor, or in the lowlands, you measure distances by miles, but when you start considering hill-trekking, then it is better to think in terms of hours. Distances can be calculated from the distance scale on the map, or you can purchase a map-measurer in any sports shop, or you can use the string method.

For this last method, you take a piece of household string and stretch it out along the intended path. Keep as close to the actual route as you can, following each twist and turn. Then measure your string against the scale on the map. Work in lengths of about 3 miles and you will have greater accuracy at the end of the day. Be sure you use the right scale.

Count every contour line that you cross and note the height. Do not assume that reaching a 3,000 feet hill-top from 1,000 feet starting point means just 2,000 feet of ascent. At some time the path may go downwards for a stretch, and then you will have to climb those lost feet again. In some instances your route may even double the amount of vertical feet you have to climb.

For your first trip, allow an hour for every 3 miles plus an hour for every 1,000 feet of ascent. This is including time for rests, meals and admiring the view.

On a day in the hills, a lightly-laden walker (for instance someone who is carrying just spare clothing and food for the day) *might* travel at an average speed of 3 miles per hour. If you are backpacking, however, carrying a tent and other equipment, the pace will be much slower.

The following is an example of a route in Scotland:

From Corrour Old Lodge to Col	1 mile	20 mins.
	21 contours	63 mins.
	Total:	83 mins.
To Carn Dearg	½ mile	10 mins.
	7 contours	21 mins.
	Journey time:	1 hr. 54

As you can see, we have covered 1½ miles and taken just over 1¾ hours, which is a long long way below 3 m.p.h. average. Other details can be added to your 'route card'. This route card will contain notes on features and compass bearings, so that you do not have to work out the details on the way, or consult the map so often. Always work out your route beforehand with map references and magnetic bearings, and make out a route card. Get one of your companions to check your workings, as it is very easy to make mistakes.

One important point is to note the estimated time of arrival at each main feature. You will know immediately if you are getting too far behind your schedule, or going too fast, which is almost equally unwelcome.

Never hurry. That is not the way to walk in the hills, for it uses up too much effort. Do not be reluctant to turn back when your intended time has elapsed. Always have an alternative destination, route, or cut-out, in mind. Pressing on regardless of time, weather or fatigue, is a certain way of getting into trouble. Fatigue destroys the rhythm of walking, which is essential if you are to cover ground easily. Even walking downhill is no rest cure, especially when you are tired. Walking downhill is not like riding a bicycle or driving a car, it is not easier going down than going up. Quite often the reverse is the case. Downhill travel can be tedious because you must be very careful where you are putting your feet, and need to be extra careful not to overstep. The jerking and bumping you set up if you hurry downhill may result in a twisted knee or ankle. In any case, where your route is over very steep ground, the downhill return journey will take *longer* than the 3 m.p.h. average expected on flat ground. Take this into consideration when planning your 'route card'.

ROUTE CARDS

For most of the time you will not be able to proceed from A to B in a straight line. Almost inevitably you will have to walk in a series of legs, to get round a river, reach a bridge or ford, avoid a marshy field or some such obstacle.

It will save much time and trouble if you prepare your route in advance by noting the legs on a **route card.**

You can draw up these easily for yourself, and note down as much information as necessary, but a typical route card looks like this:

Sheet No: 184 Start: Farm 896401 Finish: Hill 912442 Mag.Var. 8°				
Start	Mag°	Finish	Distance	Time
896401	88°	Barn 909403	2 Km	45 mins.
909403	48°	Church 916411	1 Km (by track)	20 mins.
916411	Map	Church 925424	3 Km.Rd./F.pth	45 mins.
925425	Map	Tumulus 920432	1 Km—uphill	30 mins.
920432	326°	Hill 912442	1 Km	20 mins.
	TOTAL	DISTANCE	8 Km (5 miles)	160 mins. 2 hrs. 40. say: 3 hrs.

A route card is the ideal way for groups of hill-trekkers to set out their map reading problems or instructions. Leave a copy of your route card behind, as a safety precaution should you get lost or stranded.

People can walk the route in various ways and it provides the walkers with all the necessary information, and, by setting it out in this way, forces them to consider problems of time, distance and difficulty of terrain. If you get stuck and have to retrace your route you can convert the bearings into back bearings and, using a watch come back in timed stages.

REGULAR RESTS

An estimate of the time you will be walking in the hills should also include resting time. In summer this may be 10 minutes each hour, but if the weather is very cold then just a few moments break in the walk may be a better idea. You don't want to cool down, or fall behind schedule.

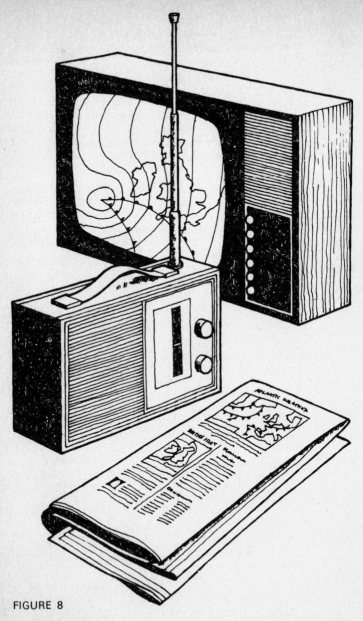

FIGURE 8

32

Chapter 5

BE WEATHERWISE

The weather is the main element controlling the success or otherwise of a hill-trekking expedition. The only weather forecast you should believe is the one that tells you it's going to be worse than at present. Get the best forecast you can and believe the worst it tells you. After all, the only certain thing in the hills is that the weather is changeable. Good weather is a bonus for most of the time, and the worst should always be anticipated. Follow that creed and you will not get yourself into too much bother. Weather conditions in British hills, especially in the winter months, can be more severe than those found in the Alps, unless you are ready for them, for weather is quite unpredictable. It can snow quite heavily on summer days in British hills, only to be followed, a few months later, by balmy weather in mid-winter.

You need to know the following points about the British weather before going into the hills, because they affect your progress and equipment. You can get this information from Press, Radio, or T.V. forecasts. Watch or listen for it.

Pressure: Falling temperature *usually* indicates worsening weather. If you hear that the pressure is 1,000 millibars (mb) *and falling*, then watch out. If you tap the barometer in the hotel or hostel and it falls, again, look at the weather, and look out your waterproofs.

Temperature: Temperature usually drops as you go higher and can alter by as much as 5°F. for each 1,000 feet of ascent. Cooled air also contracts; it sinks and sheds moisture, which is why it rains more near the mountain tops, while clear periods are maintained in the lee of hills. The higher, the colder, remember.

Wind: Altitude increases not only the strength of the wind but also the effects, because it is invariably colder on the hills than it is in the valleys. On the valley floor the incidence of houses, buildings and trees, as well as other natural features, gives some shelter from the wind and mitigates the full force. On high ground, such protection is not usually present, and winds become stronger and steadier, while the effect is physically more wearing. Wind speed increases the cooling effect of low temperature, especially at zero or near zero temperatures.

In strong winds stay off crests and steep slopes. With cagoule and rucksack on you present a considerable surface to the wind, and since it *can* blow you over cliff edges, it's better to keep away from them.

Rain and Mist: The loss in visibility is acute when rain falls and and even more so when mist sets in. These are the times when it is essential to know how to take and walk on a compass bearing, remembering to fix your position before the weather closes in.

Often, when this greyness sets about you, it will have an inconsistency which is disturbing. One moment you can see features a mile away, next moment it is dank and grey right down to your nose. As soon as there is even a *hint* of rain or mist you must take bearings to establish your position and give you something to march on, should you be forced to grope your way down. At such times navigate with care, take repeated bearings, if possible as you move along, and note the time, watching closely for the cairns on the path so that you do not become lost. You must be able to read contours on the map, and since visibility is restricted, you must also note the time and estimate the distance to give you an accurate reckoning of your position.

Snow: The ability to navigate on snow-covered terrain is one you will have to learn if winter trekking is to be enjoyed. Snow not only turns lots of different features into similarly-shaped objects, thus making map reading difficult—but when it freezes it becomes very dangerous underfoot.

Crampons or an ice-axe are essential. In these conditions you should be very wary of all icy slopes and slippery rocks.

FORECASTS

The weather forecasting services are, in most cases, too general to be able to predict what you can expect to meet on every local hillside. They are much more accurate, though, than the old ideas based on painful corns or cows sleeping in fields. Radio reports which tell you of increasing cloud and wind, or mention depressions, fronts, troughs, or low pressure, are not to be ignored. Broadcasting times vary, but you can check forecast times in the Radio Times.

WEATHER CENTRE

Always ring your local weather centre (see the Yellow Pages section of the Telephone Directory) for the necessary forecast. The London Weather Centre, for example, will gladly give you a forecast for North Wales.

In some areas telephone reports are variable, and most Mountain Rescue Service Headquarters post a report of local conditions. In the Lake District, some equipment suppliers post the local report daily, and at Pen-y-ghent Café, walkers in the Three Peaks district can get their forecast for the area. A similar service is often available at other centres,so look out for it, or enquire in the shops.

At other times it is essential to know which newspaper carries a local report on the appropriate day, and to have a telephone number you can ring before going out into the hills. The Police, the local airfield, or an outdoor centre, will all be happy to advise you. Don't forget to ask them.

PREPARE YOUR WEATHER FORECAST

Although you can't change the weather, you can be prepared to combat its effects by taking the right gear and *acting sensibly*—which may mean not going out at all. What you must avoid is arriving at a location and, finding that the weather forecast is poor, going out regardless. The attitude that having made the trip, or spent the rail fare or petrol money in getting there, you are going to bash on with it, is the attitude that brings the helicopters out!

This does NOT, incidentally, mean abandoning your trip, but appreciating the weather conditions, which will lead you to take the right gear, the right food, and to make the right decisions.

Get *two* people to assemble all the data, and prepare a forecast for the whole party for the proposed trip. Not what the data *says* but, what it *means*.

Let *two* people prepare separate forecasts and accept the worst. Always assume that, within reason, the worst forecast will be the right one. You will then be prepared, and if the forecast proves to be wrong, at least you will have erred on the right side.

As we have seen, weather comes in waves. What you are interested in, is establishing a weather pattern for the area in which you are walking. To do this you must have information for SEVERAL DAYS PRECEDING THE TRIP. The easiest way to assemble this information is to prepare a chart.

	10th	11th	12th
Gen. Forecast	Poor	Improving	Fair
Local Forecast	Snow	Rain	Clear (Frost)
Temperature	−3°C	+4°C	−3°C
Pressure	988°C	994°C	1,005°C
Sky	Low Stratus	Clearing	Clear
Wind	E/Strong	E/Falling	E/Light
Precipitation	Snow showers	Rain	Showers
T.V. Forecast	Poor	Improving	Fair
Newspaper	Poor	Poor/Improving	Improving/Fair
Local	Poor	Better	Better
Decision	Stay	Go	Go

This is a typical chart for a weekend trip hill-trekking in North Wales. The sub-headings are arbitrary, but they will, if allowed, give you a good idea of what you may expect on the weather front.

You can get all the above information from published or broadcast sources. DON'T IGNORE THE WEATHER whatever you do.

Of course, you may live in Kent and the weekend may be in North Wales. Ring your local weather centre and they will tell you what is happening in the days preceding your proposed trip, even far away up there in mountain country. Radio forecasts, being right up to date, are among the most useful.

Let us say that you have decided to go, and eventually arrive at your starting point. Ask someone there, preferably someone likely to know, what they think the weather will do over the next few days. Local information is vital, for in the U.K. the weather is subject to much local variation.

Local Police Stations, sports gear shops, Mountain Rescue Centres, local airfields and newspaper offices, all have staff who can give excellent advice. Get the local information and decide what to do. On the basis of early forecasts you can usually make a different trip from the one you intended, if the original one would be impossible in such weather. Always have alternative destinations in mind if the weather prevents you from moving on to the original one.

However, once you are out, you won't get the daily papers or see television, but you must up-date your forecasts as often as possible. Weather patterns, especially locally, can change very quickly. If you have a small, light, transistor radio, you can take it with you and can probably pick up weather reports—you must note the broadcasting times beforehand. Remember that many foreign radio sets cannot pick up Radio 4, so check that your transistor has the relevant U.K. wavelengths. See local newspapers for broadcasting times. Ask people you meet what the latest weather forecast is, but *most important*, use your eyes and common sense. The more relevant information you can collect, and the more you are prepared for it, the safer you will be.

WHAT TO DO WHEN THE WEATHER TURNS NASTY

When bad weather blows, the decision on what to do is for you to make. Moving on when conditions are bad could result in further problems, like being lost when the weather clears. If you have to make a return journey along the same path, it might be better to sit tight for a while, then move back later. Remember that darkness falls much more quickly when the cloud cover is low, and in mid-winter it might never get really light until mid-morning and be almost dark again by 3.00 p.m. Remember that you will move a lot slower in bad visibility, and even more so when it is almost dark. This will affect your timings, so remember to allow for it. As you can see, it's not just the cold, rain, and wind you have to contend with.

During the summer, which is the time when the bulk of hill-trekkers practise their sport, while the weather may be generally favourable, even good weather has a few disadvantages. The effects of heat when hill-walking can be as severe, in their way, as those of winter cold. In uphill travel it is necessary to expend energy in the form of heat and sweat, which can be quite exhausting.

Opening your shirt front, and wearing light flapping clothes is one way of dissipating some of this body heat; sweating should also be welcomed, for this is one way by which the body cools itself. You can, of course, wear shorts, but unless you are very tanned, keep your shirt on. Carrying a rucksack on skinned shoulders is a painful pastime!

Making steady progress, and not hurrying, is important. Aim for an even pace. The cooling effect of wind or breeze will be felt when you stop, and it is important at such times to select a sheltered place so that you do not get chilled, and if you cool down too much put on a sweater.

It is very important to drink enough liquid to replenish fluid lost by respiration, perspiration and other body functions. In a normal day you will drink several pints of liquid, but when it has been hard, hot going, this could be increased by as much again, if you can get it. You should try not to drink until really thirsty. Once you start you will want to keep on, and besides, cold water on a very hot day can cause stomach cramps.

On most hills the surface streams are pure providing there are no buildings upstream. Spring water is clean enough to drink from the source, but you should be wary of water standing in pools where animals may have tainted it. Carrying your drink is hard work, even in a light-weight container, but carrying water may be necessary in case the hill streams have dried up.

Salt requirements are usually adequately catered for in your normal diet, but in very hot weather, when you are sweating for hours each day, then a little extra salt in your food will balance the depletion. It is unlikely that you will need to take salt tablets in this country, but if you get cramp in the leg muscles, a little salt in a cup of water will help.

Chapter 6

COPING WITH COLD

The much shorter days of winter mean you have to know where you are going and how long the journey will take. Never venture into the hills at all in winter without adequate equipment, and certainly not without spare clothing, day-rations, torch, whistle, compass and map. In really cold weather, a sleeping bag and a survival bag would be sensible additions to your daily kit as a safety measure, even if you have no intention of staying out—you hope!

DON'T GO OUT INTO THE HILLS IN WINTER ON YOUR *OWN*.

Wind, rain, freezing fog, snow and ice are all possible in winter hill-walking. Add a blizzard or two and the certainty of slippery paths, and you have all the necessary ingredients to make the venture hazardous. But it need not be dangerous if you keep your wits about you and think out each move. Preparation is the keynote.

CLOTHING

First of all, apart from the clothing, and underclothing, which a hill-walker normally wears, you must have some thicker or warmer over-garments. Two thin sweaters are much better than one thick one, but two thick ones are better still. However, you must not be so warm that you sweat as you walk. Wear garments which can be adjusted for ventilation at the neck, because damp garments lose their heat-retaining qualities (Figure 9).

A down-filled garment, or one of the newer fibre-fill items, will offer better insulation and be lighter, if a bit bulky.

Duvet: A duvet is a garment designed for mountain wear and a waistcoat-style duvet worn beneath your anorak will keep you much warmer. Full duvets are expensive but, with a hood, they become the very best warmth preserver you can buy. A heavy-weight neoprene-coated cagoule or jacket will give better wear than thinner polyurethane-coated nylon garments. The pressure from wind will blow a thinner garment close to your body and cause you to chill more quickly.

Balaclavas: Worn rolled up as a hat, the balaclava can be rolled down over the face and ears to give more warmth when needed. You lose about 30% of your body's heat from the head, so to stay warm, keep the head covered.

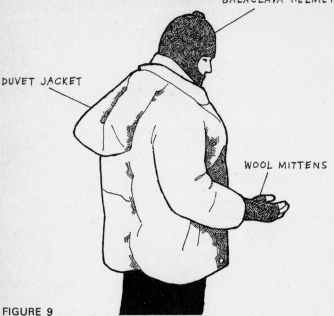

BALACLAVA HELMET

DUVET JACKET

WOOL MITTENS

FIGURE 9

Gloves: A good pair of woollen mittens are essential. If you wear gloves do not have those which are lined with imitation lamb's wool or have leather on the palms. When these get wet they are very cold, unlike wool which retains much more warmth even when wet. A pair of water-proof over-gauntlets are useful. They keep the wrists covered and as the blood runs near the skin at the wrists, this helps keep the blood warm and circulating.

FOOD AND DRINK

Food is fuel. It keeps you warm and keeps you going. In winter, you should carry a small flask of hot drink, even on a short trip. If you are going to be out all day, then take a pint-size flask filled with hot coffee or tea. Hot Oxo or Bovril may be to your liking, but whatever the drink make sure that the container will really do its job and keep the liquid piping hot.

The food which you take for a day in the hills in winter should be fully prepared before you go. There is no time out there to spread sandwiches, cut cheese, or boil eggs. A food pack should also include some chocolate and possibly something like fudge or Mars bars.

How to Eat: Eat regularly. You will be burning calories in walking and keeping warm. So eat sensibly. Start with a good breakfast, and nibble at regular intervals. For a weekend trip take lots of soups and high calorie foods. You will need more food in the winter than you would for a similar trip in the summer.

SHELTER

When looking for somewhere to rest, make sure that it is in a protected area where you will not have to face cold winds or be otherwise exposed to rapid heat loss. When you stop put on another sweater or zip up the anorak.

When you stop, do not sit on the ground or rocks. The rucksack will insulate your bottom from the cold, or you can even carry a small square of insulating mat (bought from any camping shop) which is not only going to keep you warm, but will not let the damp through either.

If you do have to remain in an exposed position, put on any waterproofs you may be carrying, for they will then prevent rapid heat loss and protect your body from the wind. Keep your back to the wind and it will help if you can find shelter, even behind your rucksack. You will find that folds in the ground or the sides of peat banks break the wind slightly and can give you a warmer spot when stopping. These are places to look out for as you are walking along just before meal-times, or for your hourly break. **Remember—always get out of the wind.**

ICE

It may not always be possible to avoid walking on ice-covered paths. When you met them, evaluate the position regarding possible hazards should you lose your footing. Say to yourself, "What will happen if I slip?" If it looks dodgy, consider the following: Is there a way round the area? Can you retrace your steps? If you slip where will you fall? Have you any aids such as rope, crampons or ice-axe?—**You should have; and a companion as well!**

If you can retrace your steps, and this is acceptable, then do so—it is safer and better than being sorry or injured. Consider always that if there is a route round the area, will the path be clear after that? Don't bash *on* if you can't get *back*.

FIGURE 10

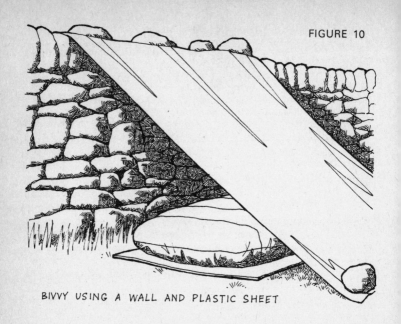

BIVVY USING A WALL AND PLASTIC SHEET

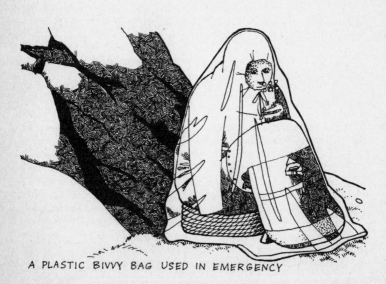

A PLASTIC BIVVY BAG USED IN EMERGENCY

Chapter 7

CAMPING IN THE HILLS

When you go day-walking in the hills, your route is usually worked out to bring you back to base, or to some night-time destination. Base may be the local inn where you are staying, or it might be a Youth Hostel, or your car in some wayside halt.

In the winter, when days are shorter, the necessity to return to base can mean that only short distances can be covered. On the other hand, in summer, when paths are busier it will take quite a while to get away to the quiet areas. At times like these the walker who has the necessary camping equipment can spend a night on the hills and really enjoy himself.

There are three main ways in which to stay out in the hills. Firstly, you can camp with a tent, which is easy and gives you tremendous independence. Secondly, you can find shelter under rocks and use a plastic or bivvy bag. This is a favoured method when the weather is mild and dry, but is useful, or even essential, in emergencies. Bivvying is a technique that all outdoor people should learn. Thirdly, you could use mountain bothies or huts, although these are not numerous. Bothies are stone huts, usually found in the Scottish hills.

Let's go through these three methods, leaving the most common till last.

BIVVYS

Constructing a windbreak or shelter from natural materials, or the use of a plastic bivvy bag or a waterproof sheet, which costs around £1.50, and keeps out the cold and damp, is called bivvying. First, you need a sheltered spot under or beside rocks. You can also use a hollow in the heather, or any spot which is sheltered from the wind (Figure 10).

Any spot will be more comfortable if you have an insulating pad (Karrimat from Karrimor or the Supamat from Berghaus). A lightweight down sleeping bag, about $2\frac{1}{2}$ lbs. in weight, will prevent you from feeling cold in even the worst conditions. 'Lightweight' only refers to the weight, incidentally, not to the insulating qualities. If you intend to bivvy a lot, though, a down bag is less suitable, as it loses its insulation properties when wet and muddy. The alternative is a man-made fibre bag.

You will probably need to wear some of your spare clothing. Wear your dry clothing at night, and put on your damp clothes again in the morning. It's grizzly to start with, but once you get moving it's not too bad.

If you are planning to spend a night out, take a small stove for brewing tea or coffee. The sort of stove to take is a Camping Gaz S.200, an Epigas Back-packer, or a lightweight one from the Vango or Lytham ranges. Just one small alloy billy and a pot-grab would be sufficient for cooking in this overnight situation.

Most hill-trekkers only bivvy in an emergency, and at such times it is always better to have remembered to carry the basic items for winter hill-trekking, of sleeping bag, bivvy bag, and emergency food, rather than try and muddle along somehow, with what you have in your pockets.

BOTHIES

A bothy is a mountain refuge, found in remote areas. Usually built of stone they have room for several people to shelter. The basic ones have little more than roof, walls and a door, and none are remotely luxurious, but for the hill-walker they are ideal. They are marked on maps, and you can get lists from outdoor organizations. Bothies are often built and maintained by mountaineering people, local climbing clubs, or Service groups. Intended for be-nighted travellers they should always be used with thought and discretion—the next person along may be in more need of shelter than yourself. If you have any spare food in tins or packets, leave it behind for the next lot.

The bothy offers shelter from the elements, so you will survive inside well enough unless it is extremely cold. Having a sleeping bag, kit and food with you, means that you can even get comfortable.

Planning to stay in a bothy overnight, means carrying a stove, food and water. You may, with luck, find some food left by other walkers, perhaps even a stub of candle and maybe some reading matter to see you through bad weather.

CAMPING

The walker who sets off into the hills carrying a tent and other essential camping gear, is going to be very independent. But his equipment is naturally going to be heavier and bulkier than the walker out for just a day, or a single night.

The *minimum* equipment would be:—

RUCKSACKS

A framed rucksack with several side pockets and a divided main compartment suits the hill-trekker's needs best (Figure 11).

Typical manufacturers of such rucksacks are Camptrails, Karrimor, Brown Best and Berghaus. These are the most popular and reliable, although many other imported makes are sold by high street shops. Go to a good outdoor outfitter and make sure the frame fits you. It depends more on the length of your back rather than your overall height. A nylon pack is lightest. It is waterproofed by a coating on the nylon, but you can still expect the seams to leak, so treat them with Copydex or seam-sealant to stop that happening. Wrapping everything in plastic bags before packing into the rucksack will stop the rain affecting the contents.

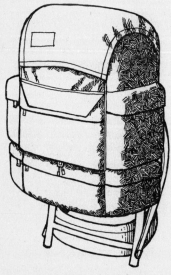

CAMP TRAILS PONDEROSA

KARRIMOR ANNAPURNA

FIGURE 11

TENTS

There are no short cuts to comfort when you start using a tent in the high places. It has to withstand much more wind and a lot more rain than on the valley floor. A mountain tent should be in two parts, with an inner and a flysheet. Single skin tents are useful for one-night outings, but can present difficulties through being saturated by condensation. Condensation is caused by the cold night air outside reacting against the warmth set up inside the tent by cooking and your body. The amount of condensation that forms inside the tent depends a lot on ventilation. You won't be able to cut out condensation completely, but you can minimise it. It is clear that on a windy night there will be less damp forming than when the air is still and your tent is pitched among the mists, so try and get a pitch with some minimal air flow, rather than a damp hollow.

Your mountain tent must be pitched to withstand strong winds. It must be a model which can be erected when the wind is blowing and preferably one where the inner tent can be put into position after the flysheet is pitched. In high winds, one of you can lie on the tent while the other gets the pegs in. Excellent mountain tents are manufactured by such firms as Robert Saunders, Fjallraven, Vango, Karrimor, Ultimate Equipment, and Blacks.

The best tent shape for hill use is the one which will easily shed the wind, and the wedge shape has become the most popular of these types. Wedge-shaped tents are made for mountain use by Karrimor, Robert Saunders and Ultimate Equipment. In this type the tent is pitched, with the small end towards the wind. Guylines are used to hold the tent secure, and strong pegs are needed. You may need to pile rocks on the pegs, or around the tent flaps, to hold it down.

A selection of pegs should be carried so that all ground conditions can be handled. A lot of mountain pitches have only a thin layer of soil over the rock, and at such times you will need to use weighty rocks on the pegs to hold the tent in place. On boggy ground, long plastic pegs are ideal. You can never have too many lengths of guyline in use when conditions are really rough. Double-guying is a useful precaution.

Inside the tent you will have room for cooking and sleeping. The sleeping area, the inner tent, must have a sewn-in groundsheet which is waterproof. The door to the inner can be zipped shut when necessary (Figure 12).

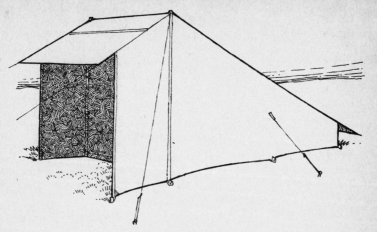

KARRIMOR MARATHON MK II

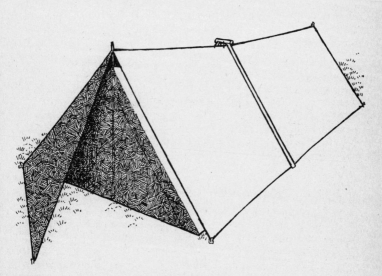

FJALLRAVEN TERMO G66

FIGURE 12

47

COOKING IN THE TENT

DON'T—if you can avoid it.

Use the porch rather than lighting the stove inside the tent. Fumes from certain stoves, or fuels, can be dangerous inside a tent or in a confined space, and if a nylon tent catches fire with you inside—disaster!

A stove which is simple to use and light to carry must be selected. Pick from methylated spirit stoves, petrol, paraffin, or gas stoves. These divide into:—

Methylated Spirits: Such as the Trangia, made in Sweden and marketed by Karrimor. It comes in two sizes and has a small fuel reservoir with two levels of burning power. The basic Trangia comes complete with billy and frypan, and other models include a kettle and a second billy.

An alternative is the Optimus Storm-Stove, made in Sweden and marketed by A. B. Optimus. This is similar in appearance and use to the Trangia.

Petrol: Pressure stoves were made famous by Primus. There are also some cheaper ones imported from the Far East. The reservoir holds petrol for nearly one hour's cooking time. You get a very fast boil, and they are easy to use once familiarity is achieved. They are fuelled with petrol or some use Meta tablets which are a form of solid fuel. Available in several versions, with or without integral windshields or billies. A sheltered cooking position is required.

Paraffin: Again, a type of stove made famous by the Swedish company, Primus. It uses paraffin from a large reservoir. A drawback is the necessity of using priming fuel to get the stove lit. Paraffin gives the cheapest form of cooking.

Butane gas: Stoves using cartridges of butane gas are popular with campers. Well-known makes include the Camping Gaz S.200 or Globetrotter; the Epigas Back-packer; the Vango range of really lightweight stoves or their preheat version; Lytham Leisure's range of stoves including the lightweight Titch; or the Primus Grass-hopper gas stove. All these are run from small disposable cartridges, using either the screw top or pierced cartridge. A sheltered cooking position is required. Butane gas, however, is affected by lowering temperatures. The use of these stoves below about 45°F is slow and tedious. Vango have improved the situation by introducing a pre-heat version which, by use of a special return tube injects heated gases back into the cartridge so that burning pressure is maintained. Cooking times are then kept to a reasonable level.

In practice, you will find that gas stoves and the methylated spirit burners will heat water to boiling point in about the same time—about 8 minutes per unit.

Petrol and paraffin pressure stoves are much quicker but need time to reach peak efficiency—about 5 minutes per pint.

The methylated spirit storm-stoves are the only ones which have uniform performance in the open or sheltered positions. Butane gas stoves need sheltered positions at all times or the boiling time is lengthened considerably. Consider the fuel factor when you are buying a stove as it may well influence your choice.

BILLIES

The cooking tins can be simple cake tins, or sophisticated stacking ones. It is better to buy those which are non-stick. The choice is large. Don't forget that a plastic mug is very useful, and won't burn your lips as a metal one can.

WATER

Your water container should be collapsible. Those which have a large opening are better as they can be more easily filled in a stream. Screw-top bottles, plastic or alloy, are ideal for carrying water during the day. You will need about 2 litres of water for an overnight stop.

SLEEPING BAG

Your sleeping bag should be the best and the lightest you can afford. The best will have a filling of pure new down, which weight for weight, is the most efficient filling for sleeping bags. Your bag need not weigh more than 3 lbs. if it is filled with quality down.

The lightest bags are around 2 lbs. and when filled with pure new down, they can be relied on to keep you warm in all but the coldest weather. Even then, with some additional clothing you should have a comfortable night's sleep.

Down will lose its efficiency if it gets damp. Keeping your sleeping bag dry in the tent or rucksack is only half the battle, though. Body moisture emitted at night has to be purged from the bag by airing. It you have continuous wet conditions while you are camping, this can be very difficult, and for use during the winter, man-made fibres have a lot to offer.

A great deal is heard nowadays about the new man-made fillings such as Fibre-Fill II, and P.3. Used as a filling for sleeping bags they are heavier and less efficient than down. A bag for winter use which has a Fibre-Fill II filling may weigh $4\frac{1}{2}$ lbs. or more, but, if it is much bulkier, on the other hand, when it gets wet you will still be warm inside it. Damp, perhaps, but warm!

Also on the credit side you will find that you lie more comfortably in a Fibre-Fill bag as the material does not compress beneath you like down.

Sleeping bags made by the following companies have been found to be among the best:—

Banton Point Five:	— Orion
	— Helios
Mountain Equipment:	— Light-Line
	— Snowline
	— Laveredo
Blacks:	— Tromso
	— Back-packer
David Moore:	— Sno-Cap

INSULATING MATS

Your sleeping bag should be used in conjunction with an insulating mat. When you lie on these you do not feel the cold of the ground below, although they are not thick enough to be really comfortable. One great asset is that the closed-cell foam will not absorb moisture, so the damp cannot strike up at you. With an air bed, the ground chills the air inside, and this chilled air can and does absorb your body heat. On the other hand, air beds are more comfortable. Karrimat and Supamat weigh about 10 ozs. for a body-length piece of insulating matting, which will roll tightly to be carried either inside or outside your rucksack. You can get hip-length mats which are lighter, and pad the legs with spare clothing.

Brown Best have incorporated a length of insulating matting and some layers of thin foam into their 'Adsmat', which is more comfortable than the other simple mats. The Adsmat comes wrapped up in a proofed nylon bag which can serve as a stuff-sack for your sleeping bag during the day, if you cram it all in tightly.

With this equipment as your basis for camping, there is no reason why you cannot go into any of the British hills for days at a time.

Chapter 8

WHERE TO CAMP

The fells are very exposed places in which to start your outdoor experience. It would be better to make sure you know exactly how to put up your tent when there is half a gale blowing on lower ground—even in your back garden—rather than attempt it for the very first time on high peaks. You ought to make sure your experience includes erecting it in the dark also. Confine your expeditions to the lower slopes until you are ready, or as ready as you ever will be to go higher. In the end, though, you'll just have to go out and try!

A GOOD SITE

Ideally, if you can, pitch your tent near running water. Make sure that the water will not rise and cause a flood during the night. When camping next to streams in rainy weather, remember that the effects of rain on higher ground may take an hour or two, or even longer, to reach your position. Water from such streams is safe to drink providing there are no buildings upstream, or the banks are not fouled by animals. If the main stream is foul, take water from feeder streams at the sides. When camping beside lakes (lochs, tarns, llyn, mere, water or lochan) try to get your drinking water at the feeder streams rather than the main body. Never wash *in* the water of the lake or stream, but beside it.

Position: Try to get some shelter for your tent, with protection from the force of the wind. Below an outcrop of rock may be suitable, but watch out for falling stones, particularly in rain or a thaw. A fold in the ground or the lee side of a slope or the bank of a stream will give enough shelter in most cases. Ground condition is probably more important than overall position. If the ground is stony and will not take pegs, or is very damp, then even a sheltered spot should be relinquished for one where the ground is firm, but well drained.

Look for a pitch where you will be warmed by the morning sun. It is this warmth which will help to dry out the damp from a cold night, and clear the condensation from the tent.

In summer months, look for your pitch during the late afternoon, unless you want to stop earlier. In mid-winter you should know where you will put your tent at least one hour before dark.

Your day can start as early as you like, but generally you can

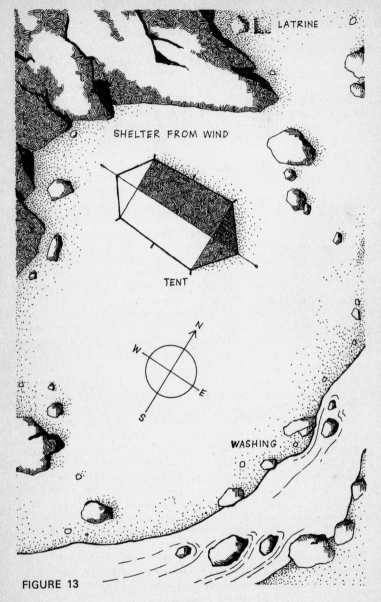

LATRINE

SHELTER FROM WIND

TENT

N
W
E
S

WASHING

FIGURE 13

expect to take an hour over getting up, having breakfast and packing away your equipment. If you are not well organised you could take double that time (Figure 13).

A TYPICAL CAMP

Having found a pitch, beside a stream on high ground, if you are lucky, try to get the early morning sun, if any. The sun rises from the east, remember. Use your compass to check this if necessary. Clear the ground if there are rocks or stones about. Get rid of any other debris, and tidy up the site.

If you have a small tent then you will appreciate a rock outcrop or open space for your kitchen area. If the weather is bad, you will cook inside the tent or in the tent porch. Make the most of the ground available; it is much easier to sit outside on a ledge or on a stump or rock, than on flat ground. You should try and be within easy access of water, as having to clamber down muddy banks into a stream is not a good idea.

Pitch your tent: If the weather is a bit wild, or your equipment and clothing is wet, it may be better to finish the cooking and other jobs while sitting under the flysheet, before putting the inner tent into place. After that, the evening routine may well go like this:—

1. Brew your tea. A brew will cheer you up and be very welcome!
2. Start supper: — Soup (packet)
   Main meal—fish or meat with potato and vegetable. Pudding, cake, biscuits or fruit
3. — Another drink
4. Turn in.

Your sleeping bag should be unrolled and fluffed out so that the down can loft (in other words, stretch out into the channels of the bag). Discard boots and wet clothing for night wear or dry clothing. Wring all the excess moisture you can from the day-time clothing. Hang it up where it will get a chance to dry without dripping on you or your other gear.

Wear moccasins, training shoes or similar light footwear, during the evening, inside the tent. Leave muddy footwear outside, under the flysheet.

By dusk, make sure you have made your tent secure against all bad weather—even if a storm is not anticipated it is better to be safe than sorry. Replenish water supplies, and put torch, shoes and sweater where you can lay your hands on them quickly. Wash any dirty dishes and fill the billy for the morning brew. In very cold weather (when water freezes) your water bottle will be useless, the narrow neck blocks solid, so keep the bottle inside the tent, where the elements can't work on it.

When the nights are really long, such as in mid-December, you will spend nearly 15 hours in your sleeping bag. Breakfast will be a long way off, so make sure your supper was a good one, or keep some chocolate or biscuits handy for a night-time snack. Don't let chocolate flakes get inside the sleeping bag; if they melt, they make a frightful mess!

MORNING ROUTINE

The first job is to get a cup of tea brewed, then have breakfast. Leave the tent up so that the condensation can dispense—sun permitting.

Breakfast should consist of:—

    Tea

    Meusli, or Porridge, or some other cereal with milk

    Scrambled egg, or fried egg with bacon

    Bread with butter, jam, honey or marmalade

Remember that in summer you may have runny butter, but in winter it will be rock-hard. Sticky foods like marmalade, honey, and jam, should be carried in a screw-top polythene bottle or container. Dried powdered milk is easier to take with you than cow's milk which may go sour. Tinned milk is good, but weighs heavily.

Pack your sleeping bag and other night gear away. Strike camp by packing your tent and other equipment and then making sure that you have left nothing behind which will show you stayed the night on this spot. Remember the Country Code and 'leave no litter.'

You will find all this much more interesting and rewarding than spending the night down in an inn or hotel on the valley floor, and then having to walk all the way back again, but the secret of successful camping in the hills is organization.

Chapter 9

HAZARDS IN THE HILLS

As I tried to point out, the best way to avoid trouble in the hills, is to have the right experience and equipment, and by always being safety-minded. Happily, the hills are usually kind, but please pay attention to the possibility of the following hazards:

STREAMS

These can vary from small trickles of water to rushing torrents. If a stream is shallow and you can see that the bottom is clear of obstructions, then well-laced boots and gaiters will keep the water out as you ford it. If it is deeper, roll up the trousers and take the socks off, but wear the boots in case you tread on something sharp. In fast-flowing water, or where you are crossing by stepping from rock to rock, it is a good idea to unfasten any waistband strap you may have on your rucksack. Then if you do fall in, it is much easier to get your rucksack off quickly. Never cross streams in spate. Head **upstream** until the course narrows and you can step across safely. Water takes the shortest route off a hill, so be very careful when following a stream downhill in mist. It may lead you over a cliff-top, and so following streams off a hill is a practice best avoided.

Unless it tastes funny, stream water in the hills is usually safe to drink. In the valleys or near farms it may well be polluted. It is always better to boil it or use purifying tablets. Water is heavy to carry, so use stream water whenever possible, if it seems safe and pure. Remember, however, that in summer the hill streams may dry up.

SCREE

These are slopes, or channels, of loose stones and small rocks, often found on steep hillsides. The scree may move as you walk over it. Scree-running can be fun, but it is hard on the boots and can be very dangerous if you go too fast, or fall. Lean backwards and be ready to sit down if you feel your feet getting trapped or your legs twisted. Sitting down on scree, even if it is moving, soon brings you to a halt. Never move faster than the speed which feels safe, and go *with* the stones as they slide. Beware of rocks or ledges in the scree, and avoid snow-covered scree in winter.

BOULDERS

Boulder fields require a firm foot. Often you can step from one small boulder to another, but beware of those which move and do be careful not to put your legs down into holes between the rocks where your foot could become trapped or your leg broken. This is a particular hazard in winter, with ice about.

FALLING ROCKS

If a boulder or rock is dislodged and starts to move downhill, shout "**BELOW**" to the people who may be in the way. If you see small rocks bounding in your direction, stoop down, or crouch really low, leaving your rucksack, or a bigger boulder, between you and the advancing danger. Don't look away, covering your eyes. If you see a large rock coming, you can usually avoid it. Cowering down won't stop a rock hitting you.

PEAT

Wet, mucky peat is a feature on many hills, and even if it is not actually at the summit you will often find that the path upwards is a slushy one. There are some hill ranges where peat is not a problem, but marshy ground and peat bogs are very good reasons why you should always have a pair of gaiters in your kit. When you come to a wet stretch on a well-worn path, there may be a few stepping stones set into the mire to help you across. At other times the path gets more boggy and on such routes, like the path up to Pen-y-ghent from Horton, it stretches wider and wider along the stream banks. Pick your path and move quickly when crossing slushy bogs. Step on to the base of clumps of reed for a little more support. Avoid the bright green patches as these are invariably deeper, and often seem to be bottomless!

ROCK FACES

Unless you have the correct equipment, the training, and the experience, do not attempt any rock climbing. Stay within the limits dictated by common sense. Hill-trekking and rock climbing are allied, but separate activities.

SNOW

In winter and spring, even on the lower slopes, you can meet snowfields or patches of ice. If you are going to venture on to, or across them at all, you need an ice-axe or crampons, and preferably both (Figure 14).

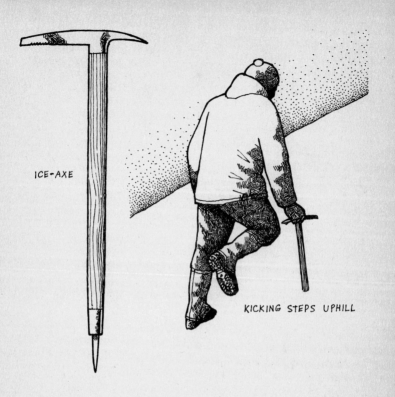

ICE-AXE

KICKING STEPS UPHILL

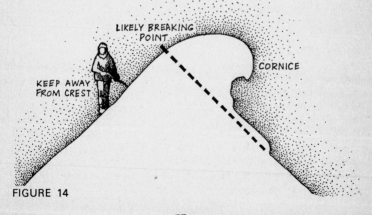

LIKELY BREAKING
POINT

KEEP AWAY
FROM CREST

CORNICE

FIGURE 14

Avoid crossing a steep grass slope covered with ice and snow patches. If you slip on it you could go all the way down. As you gain experience in the hills you can practise snow and ice techniques, like step-kicking and braking with the ice-axe, but always do so on safe slopes, where you can only fall or skid a few feet. Snow can be deep when lying in gullies, and while no sensible person, equipped only for hill-walking, will venture on snow-slopes, you may have to venture across a patch of snow, and thus get into trouble. Don't go on a snow-slope without an ice-axe. Look around and see where you could end up if you were to slip. Don't walk up to crests or cliff edges under snow. The snow may have formed a cornice, extending beyond the level of the firm ground, and collapse under you. While crossing such areas you should be roped-up.

VERGLAS
Verglas is simply ice, which can form in low temperature conditions. Mist or drizzle will freeze on rocks or mountain paths, turning normally secure footholds into slippery traps. You may not notice 'verglas' forming until you start to slide, so watch out for it.

ICE
Ice can form, and remain, in places where you would least expect to find it. Under trees, and in the lee of rocks, where the sun can't reach, may be icy, when the area round about is slushy but safe, or drying nicely.

Your body heat can first condense inside your tent, and the condensation turn into ice from the cold outside. Ice in the hills is a dangerous event, and when it is present you must be extra careful.

LIGHTNING
You can often spot lightning flickering around the hills as a storm approaches. Very rarely will you hear of people falling victim to a Jove-like thunderbolt from the clouds. Nevertheless, lightning is a hazard, and it is as well to take precautions when a thunderstorm is imminent (Figure 15).

Keep off exposed ridges, open slopes, and away from lone trees. Cover up metal objects, such as ice-axes, and if the lightning is constant, seek shelter, lie down on your rubber mattress if possible, and move away from any prominent or metal object likely to attract a strike.

FIGURE 15

ICE-AXES

While you should *always* wear the right clothing and carry the right equipment, in winter you must be particularly careful, always carrying an ice-axe, and possibly wearing crampons.

You can use an ice-axe for extra support or security, for cutting steps, and as a brake if you slip and fall.

They come in various sizes and you want one that is (just) too short to lean on like a walking stick. You can get very short ice-axes, but these are for mountaineering, climbing ice-walls and so on, not for hill-walkers. The ice-axe *must* have a stout web or leather wrist loop.

Hill-walkers should never get into the situation where they need to cut steps with the ice-axe. Step-cutting is a technique best learned on a safe slope under competent tuition.

However, in the winter you must have an ice-axe with you for safety. The greatest safety feature is the ability to use the ice-axe as a brake.

BRAKING WITH AN ICE-AXE

If you have to cross a snow slope, always use the ice-axe as the safety feature, sinking it deep in the snow, with the loop around your wrist (Figure 16).

If you do fall—and you will usually slip sideways—roll *at once* on to your chest, and drive the pick of the ice-axe into the snow, at chest level, not at arm's length. Do it fast, as you will quickly pick up speed. On ice (heaven help you!—What are you doing there?) you may find it very difficult to get the axe in.

Practise this, under instruction, or with an experienced friend, on a short smooth slope. It is quite difficult, and needs strength and skill.

CRAMPONS

Most hill-walkers wear rubber soled vibram boots, and in winter, with ice and verglas about, these are not very efficient. You need nailed boots, or crampons.

Crampons are spiked soles, that can be strapped on to your boots, giving a good grip on snow or ice.

Crampons are no good unless they fit properly, and are securely strapped. Otherwise you will quickly walk out of them, or find them flying off as you move your foot forward. Moreover, you can trip over them, or catch a spike in your other trouser-bottom. Always wear gaiters. Crampons need a bit of practice, before you get used to them.

BRAKING WITH THE ICE-AXE

FIGURE 16

NAILED BOOTS

As I've just mentioned, most hill-walkers wear rubber soled boots, and if they go on high ground in winter, then crampons are a must. However, since the weather all the year in Britain is highly unpredictable, nailed boots can serve as an alternative to crampons in winter, and as a spare pair of boots in summer. They are essential equipment for slippery rocks and muddy slopes.

*   *   *

I don't want to encourage the newcomer to hill-trekking to buy items of equipment more suited to the advanced enthusiast, or to use them as an excuse to take risks outside the scope of his experience. The point of this chapter is to stress that in winter, particularly, you must carry an ice-axe, and know how to use it. Purchase the other items and use them after learning how and when to make use of them, and not before.

HILL-TREKKER'S KIT LIST

FOR SUMMER TREKKING

CLOTHES:
Cleated, rubber-soled boots
Gaiters
Wool socks (3 pairs)
Wool-based breeches or trousers
Warm underwear
String vest
Wool shirts, pullovers
Close-woven windproof smock or anorak
Balaclava or wool hat
Cagoule

KIT:
Light frameless rucksack
Food
Map
Compass

FOR SAFETY:
Spare clothing
Whistle
Survival bag, space blanket
Spare food
Torch and spare bulb and batteries
Route card (plus one left at base)
First-Aid kit

FOR STAYING OUT:
Light tent
Sleeping pad or Adsmat
Stove
Sleeping bag
Large, framed rucksack
Water

In late autumn, winter and spring, you must *add* to this list as follows:—

FOR WINTER TREKKING

CLOTHES:
Summer scale of gear, plus:
Warm underwear
Duvet jacket
Over-trousers
Nailed boots
Gloves and waterproof over-mitts

KIT:

Summer scale of gear, plus:
- Ice-axe
- Crampons
- Extra food (prepared beforehand)
- Warm prepared drink

FOR SAFETY:

Summer scale of gear, plus:
- One or more companions
- Tent
- Stove
- Flares or smoke candles

FOR STAYING OUT:

Summer scale of gear, plus:
- A mountain tent, with flysheet
- Sustaining food
- Experience in day-trekking

Rather than spend a lot of cash buying gear you may not need, it is best to buy in bits and pieces, as your experience and skill urges you to trek ever higher, and later in the year. Joining an organization like the Backpackers' Club can provide the solitary walker with amiable companions, who will share his ideals and contribute to his experience.

Whatever you do, enjoy yourself—and see you, sometime, up on the hills!